The Nail technician's Career Guide

Andy Hai Dinh

Published by Andy Hai Dinh, 2023.

Also by Andy Hai Dinh

Acrylic and Dipping Powder - Product Knowledge and Applications
The Nail technician's Career Guide
A Beginner's Guide to Trading - Stock and Forex Technical Analysis
Win More, Trade Better - A Practical Guide to Trading and Investing
Win More, Trade Better - A Practical Guide to Trading and Investing

Watch for more at https://pensight.com/x/lona.

Table of Contents

The Nail Technician's Career Guide:
The Blueprint to A Successful Nail Salon Business

ISBN: 9798868090080

Cover design by: Andy Hai Dinh

Library of Congress Control Number: 2018675309

Printed in the United States of America

ABOUT THE AUTHOR

Andy Hai Dinh, an established nail artist and educator, has been active in the US nail industry since 2004. His nail works have gained more than 2.8 million views on Google and 23k followers on Instagram (@andyhaidinh). Over the years, he has managed some of the most successful nail salon businesses in Southern California.

Andy Hai Dinh is the founder of LONA - Life of Nails Academy - an online platform for nail training courses and nail resources.

He is currently working as a market researcher and nail salon consultant. Andy is also a trader who profits from swing-trading stocks and Forex currencies.

CHAPTER 1: TECHNICAL TIPS

Natural Nail Preparation

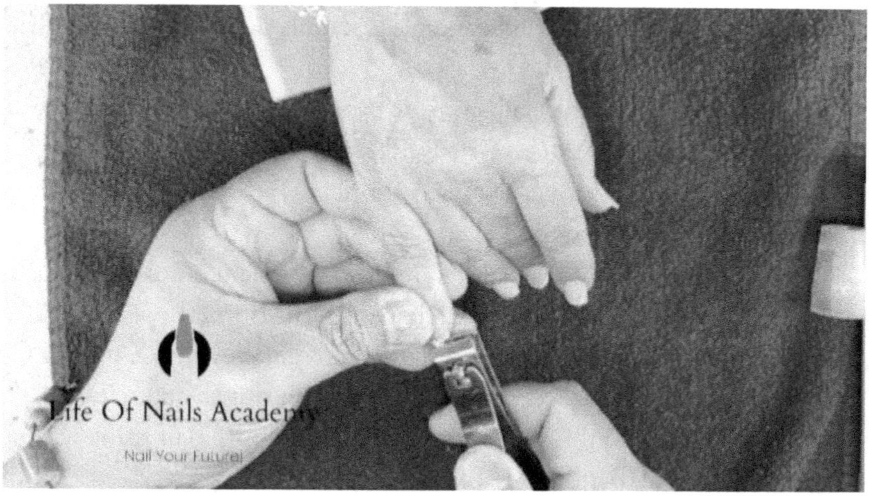

•Always wash your hands and let your clients wash their hands with soap prior to any nail service.

• Always trim natural nails as short as possible and round off nail corners prior to the application of tip extensions.

•Always push back the cuticles with the rounded end of a cuticle pusher and remove dead tissues and nail shine with a Fine Paper Sanding band with electric file (E-File) at 4K RPM (round per minute) prior to product application.

•To completely remove all oil traces from the nail after nail shine removal, cleanse nails with lint-free nail wipes and alcohol.

•For Acrylic, Structure Gel, Poly Gel and Gel Polish applications, sparingly apply an Acid Nail Primer onto the natural nails after tip extensions application and tip blending. Sparingly apply a second coat of Acid Primer on nails of clients who have experienced more product lifting problem in previous servicing sessions.

•If using an Acid-Free Primer, do apply it generously onto the natural nails to ensure adhesion between the nails and the product.

•When filing the natural nails, use only 150 Grit or 180 Grit Nail Files.

•When removing nail shine, it is possible to substitute a Fine Paper Sanding Band with a 240 Grit Buffer Block.

•For Cuticle Care prior to Artificial Enhancement Nail services, perform a Dry Manicure.

•Dry Manicure Procedure: Trim and shape natural nails. Push back cuticles. Use Cone Shape Cuticle Nail Drill Bit and E-File at 6K RPM to file under and lift the cuticles up. Trim cuticles with a pair of Cuticle Nippers or Cuticle Scissors. Buff to smooth out the cuticles with a Ball Shape Cuticle Nail Drill Bit at 8K RPM. Remove nail shine with a Fine Paper Sanding Band at 4K RPM.

•Avoid performing a Water Manicure prior to Artificial Nail Enhancement services. Soaking natural nails for several minutes in water and using cuticle softener solution on client's nails will negatively impact the adhesion between artificial nail products and the natural nails.

•First Aid Procedure: If you accidentally nick the surrounding skin or the cuticle of your client's nail and it bleeds, stop the service immediately. Let client wash hands with soap. Apply a Liquid Styptic such as Infa-Lab Magic Touch to the cut to stop the bleeding. Use a Q-Tip soaked in alcohol to carefully cleanse any excess of the liquid styptic off the nail plate without touching the wound. Resume service.

Nail Tips Applications

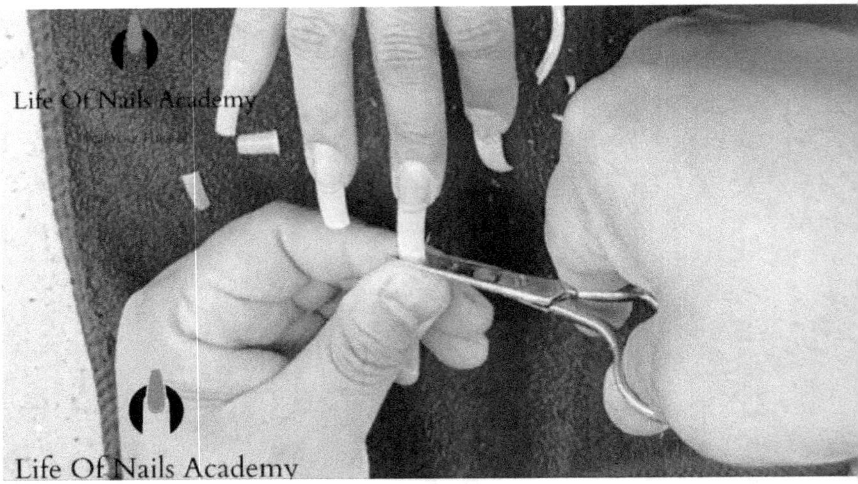
Life Of Nails Academy
Life Of Nails Academy

•For short extensions, use only natural curve stock nail tips.

•For longer artificial enhancement, use specialty tips (pre-shaped nail tips) to reduce tip shaping time.

•When applying nail tips, start with the pinky nail of your

client's right hand. Choose the correct tip size for each nail (fit nail exactly from side wall to side wall) and get out of the tip box two tips for each nail so that you will have ready all the tips for your client's left hand as well. If a certain tip size doesn't fit a nail perfectly, choose a tip one size larger and file the sides to reduce width.

•Only apply one drop of nail glue to each of the nail tip wells to avoid excess glue getting onto client's skin.

•Nail Glue will dry much slower in cooler room temperature. To speed up the glue drying process, brush some Activator solution (bottle #3 of dip nail system) or Acetone onto each tip of the natural nails prior to applying plastic tips with nail glue.

•When apply plastic nail tips, make sure your client's hand is stabilized and on an even plane - not pointing down or up and not tilting left or right.

•Whenever possible, use the same nail tip size for index, middle and ring fingernails.

•When choosing nail tips for extensions, take out 2 nail tips for each nail of the right hand. For most clients, pinky nails are usually sizes 10, 9 or 8. Index, middle and ring fingernails are 7, 6, 5 or 4. Thump nails are 3, 2, 1 or 0. Of course there will always be exceptions. But remembering this guideline will help you save time during tip extensions application.

•To apply nail tips straight, visualize and line up the nail tips with the central line running through the knuckles of the fingers.

•Only glue nail tips onto the nails as deep as the nail tip wells are (about 1mm). Do not cover too much natural nails with plastic tips. Most nail products are formulated to bond with natural nails. The less natural nail surface there is for the product to bond with, the easier the product will pop off or peel off after polymerization.

•Store your unused nail glues in the refrigerator to prevent them from drying up. Heat, lighting, or natural sunlight exposure can negatively affect many nail products.

•When using pre-shaped tips for long Square, Coffin, or Stiletto nails, avoid filing the side walls to re-shape the tips. They were made in perfect shapes to reduce perimeter filing time. After tip application and tip blending, you should apply Nail Primer and proceed with product application.

•When using natural, curve stock tips, use a pair of small, straight, and pointed scissors to trim nail tips into desired shape if necessary.

•For nail shapes with straight side walls such as Square, Coffin and Stiletto, there is no need to file the tips after trimming them into desired shape.

•For Square shape, cut tips across at 1mm longer than final nail length to compensate for filing.

•For Round or Oval shape, cut tips 1mm longer than final length. Diagonally trim off a small part of both corners. Use 120 Grit nail file to round off the tip ends.

•For Coffin shape, cut tips 1mm longer than desired length and trim both sides diagonally so that the width of the tip ends will be about 1/3 of the width of the natural nail beds.

•For Stiletto shape, cut tips exactly at final nail length. Trim both sides diagonally from a central point on the tip ends to create a pointy shape. For a proper Stiletto shape, the length of the tip extensions should be at least twice the length of the natural nail beds.

•For Classic Almond shape, cut tips 2mm longer than final length. Trim both sides to create a pointy shape. Cut away 2mm of the points.

Use 120 Grit nail file to round off the tip ends.

•For Pointed Almond shape, cut tips at final length. Trim both sides diagonally to create the pointy shape. Unlike Stiletto shape, Pointed Almond shape can be much shorter and have a slight curve on each side of the tips.

•For Tapered Square shape, cut tips 1mm longer than final length. Trim both sides so that the width of the tip ends will be 4/5 of the width of the natural nail beds.

•After nail tip application, use a Fine Paper Sanding Band and E-File at 6K RPM to blend the tips smooth with the natural nails. Dust to remove filing dust and cleanse the nail plates with Alcohol before applying Nail Primer. Proceed with product application.

Nail Shape References

SQUARE

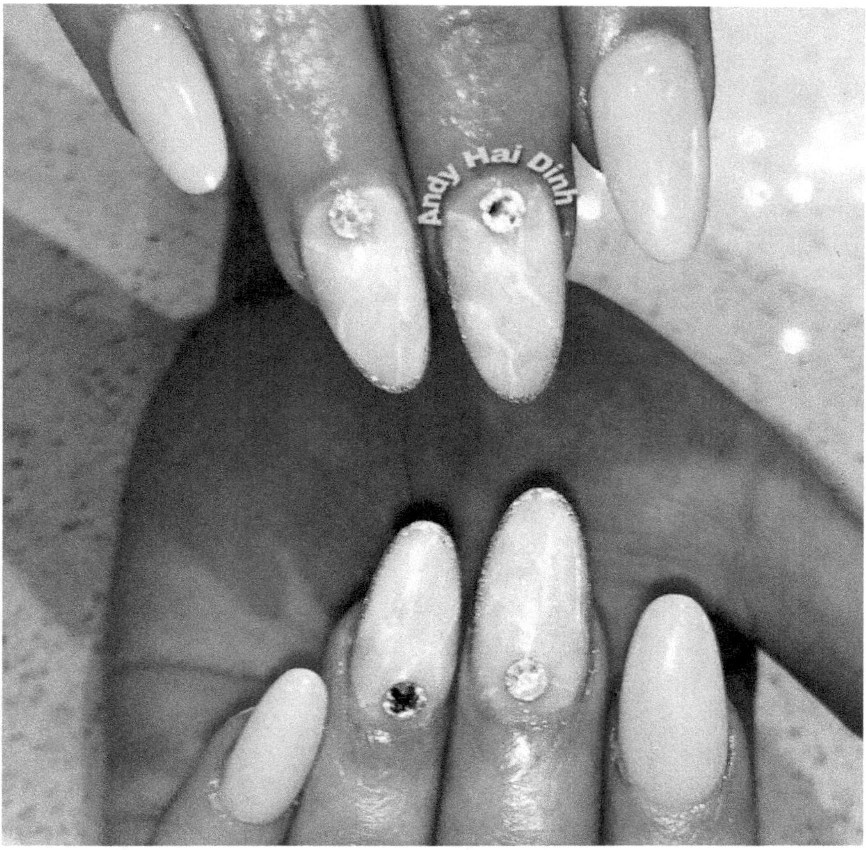

OVAL

TAPERED SQUARE

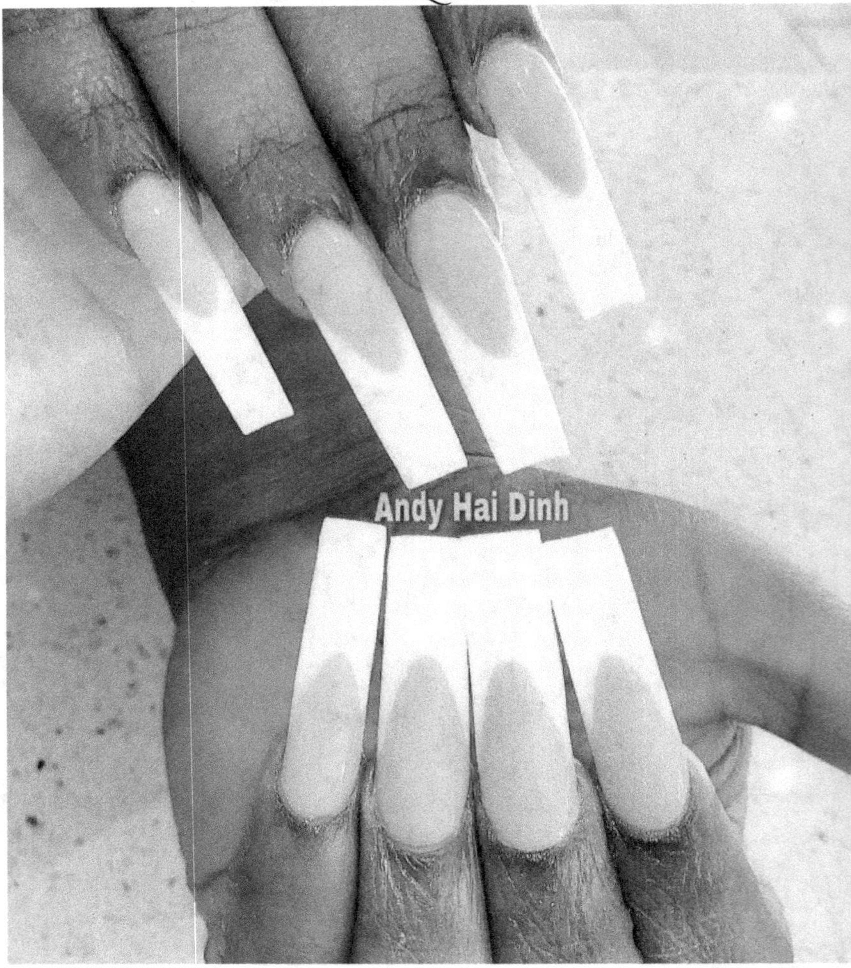

COFFIN

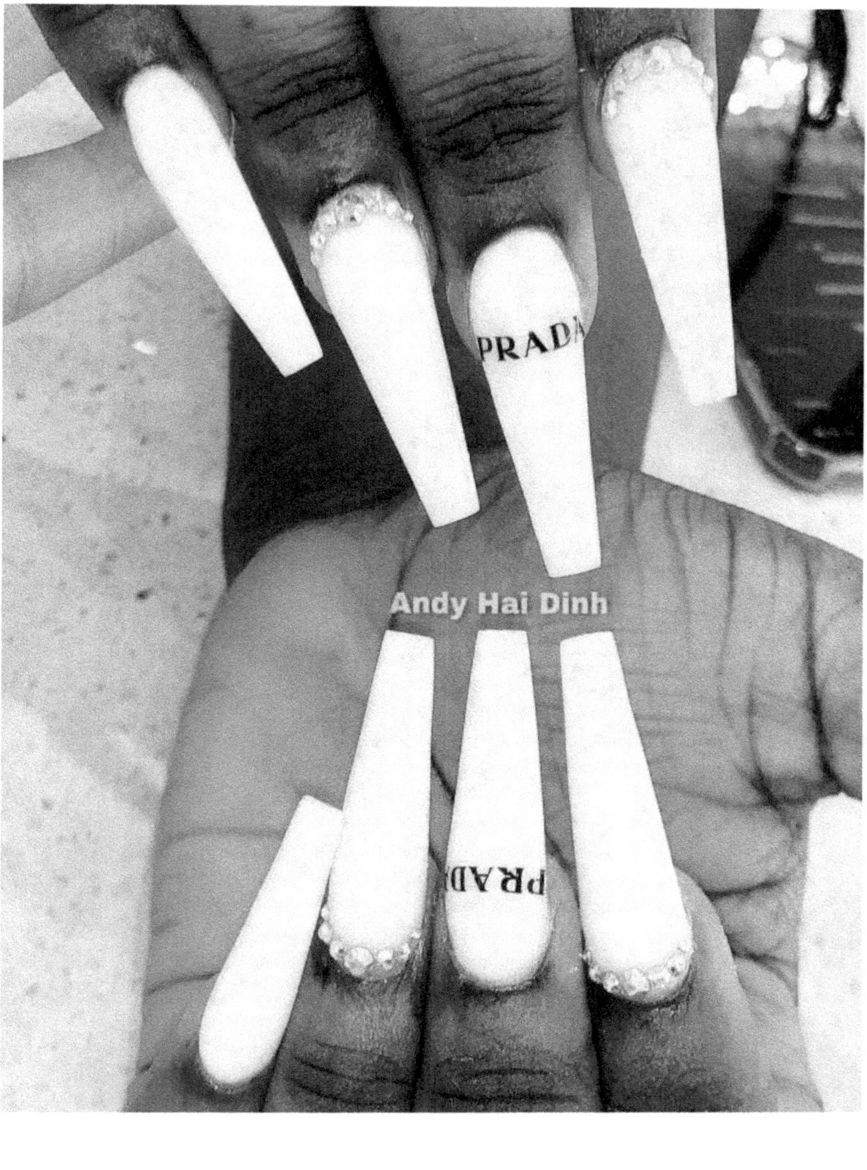

STILETTO

ALMON

Acrylic Application

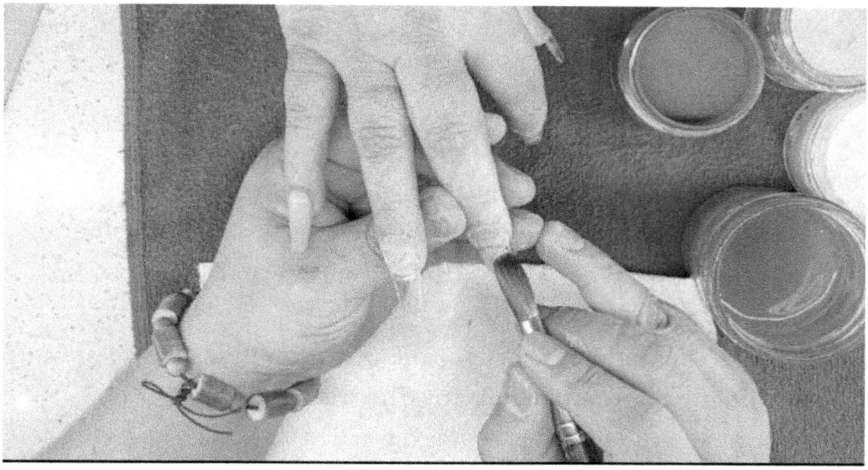

•Each type of acrylic powder will have a certain "feel" when you work with it.

•Clear, glitter and white powders tend to be runnier.

•Black powder and shimmer color powders tend to take much longer to polymerize (become fully cured).

•To help any powder polymerize quicker, after the application and before any filing, gently cleanse the nail surface with Acetone soaked in a piece of paper towel.

•EMA monomers usually come in dark purple color, less pungent and work best in room temperature between 72*F and 76*F.

•EMA monomers are approved by all State Boards in the US.

•EMA monomers give you a longer working phase to manipulate the acrylic powder.

•Neon color powders and dark color powders such as purple, navy blue and burgundy can become marbleized if you fail to control the ratio between liquid and powder. Recommended ratio is often 2 parts of monomer to 1 part of powder.

•Control the amount of liquid in your acrylic brush after picking up a ball of acrylic by dapping the empty side of the brush onto a paper towel.

•MMA monomers usually come in lighter purple color, more pungent and will make acrylic powders polymerize much faster (shorter working phase).

•MMA monomers are banned in most states in the US.

•The purple dye in both EMA and MMA monomers is added to prevent the straw-colored effect (turning pale yellow) when you mix the monomers with a white or a clear powder.

•Even though there are clear monomers available in the market, they are not recommended to use

with clear or white powders.

•When working with an EMA monomer during winter season and with the working room temperature under 70*F, you can warm up the monomer by heating the liquid container on an electric cup warmer or in a bowl of hot water to improve product control.

•When working with an EMA monomer during summer season and with the working room temperature over 78*F, cooling the liquid jar in a bowl of cold water or ice cubes will give you more time to perfectly sculpt the acrylic nails.

•Adding a small amount of Acetone into EMA liquid will also make acrylic powder polymerizing faster. However, be cautious when using this method since you can compromise the integrity of the monomer by adding too much Acetone.

•Always clean your acrylic brush with EMA monomer right after each service. If the brush is clogged up, you will need to soak it in EMA monomer or a brush cleaner solution for at least 2 hours before attempting to remove the clogged acrylic in between the brush bristles.

Do not forcefully try to scrape off the dried product on the brush hair.

•Never use Acetone to clean or soak any kind of nail brushes.

•Always have several acrylic nail brushes to work with. Use brushes size 16 or 18 when working with long acrylic nails. Use brushes size 14 to work with short acrylic nails or on clients who have small nail beds. brushes size 12 to do acrylic overlays or an acrylic fill-in service.

•Always encapsulate ombre, marbled and glitter nails with clear powder.

•To prevent white powder nails from turning yellowish during application, also encapsulate them in clear powder.

•To optimize your workflow and reduce the amount of filing, you must master your acrylic applications. Always try to perfectly smooth out the acrylic surface even if you must continue adding on more product.

•For detailed video instructions on acrylic applications, filing techniques and acrylic nail art, check out my online courses at: "pensight.com/x/lona".

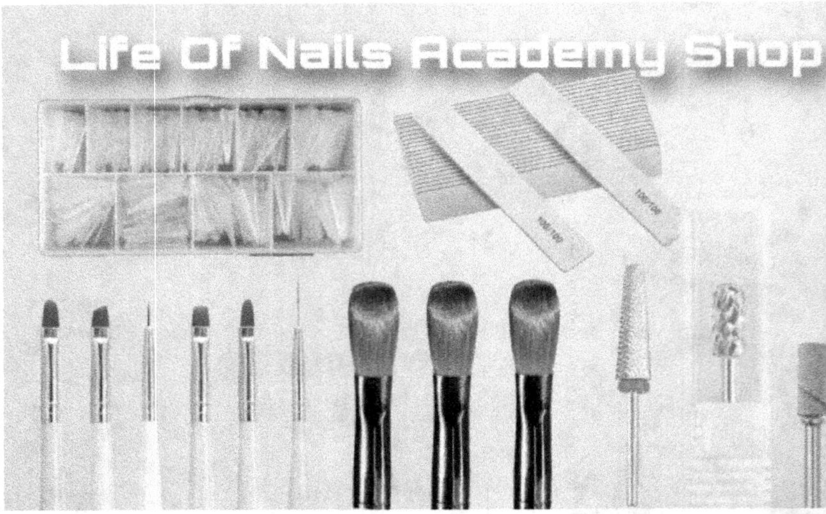

•For selected nail tools and nail accessories, visit "shoplona.company.site"

Hand Filing Procedure

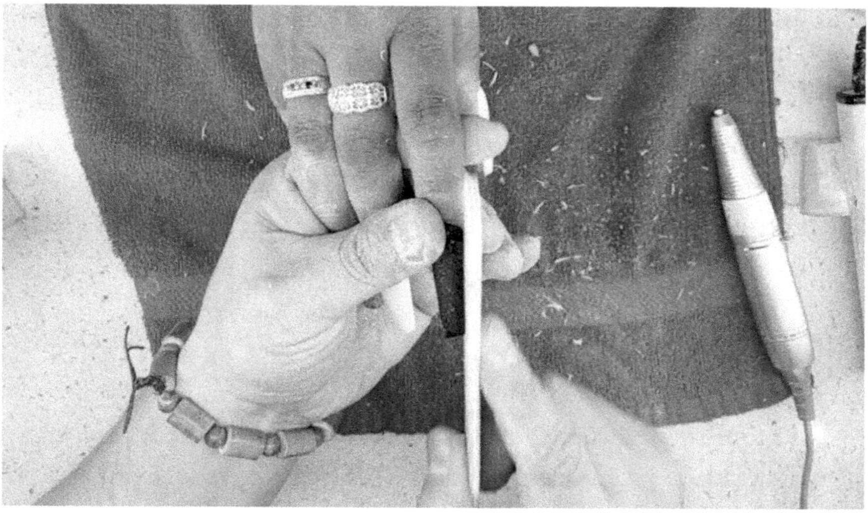

•Use 80/80 or 100/100 Grit Nail File.

•Always score a new hand file by rubbing its edges on another hand file or on the grooved area of a cuticle pusher.

•Firmly hold 1/3 of the nail file in the palm of your hand as if holding a knife.

•Step 1: Start with straightening the side walls of the nail by keeping your file square and straight against each side of the nail extension. Use long strokes and maintain pressure while filing the side walls. Give each side about 10 strokes before you pause and lift the file off the nail to observe. Do not pull away and curve the file at the very last stroke. Pause and lift the file off!

•Step 2: Hold your file vertically and square it up against the free edge. Rubbing the file up and down on the free edge to straighten it up.

Stop in between to observe before you resume filing until the tip become very square. To round off a tip end, angle your file 45* under the tip and use a rocking motion to surf left and right to create a round shape.

•Step 3: Pinch 1/3 of the nail file between the index and middle fingers of your dominant hand. Spread the thumb out and rest it on top of the nail file. Use a side-to-side rocking motion to file horizontally and smooth out Zone 3 (cuticle area) of the acrylic nail.

•Step 4: Continue to hold the nail file as above and apply the side-to-side rocking motion to file diagonally from top right corner to bottom left corner of the nail to reduce product bulk on the left side of the acrylic nail.

•Step 5: Repeat step 4 but on the opposite, from top left corner to bottom right corner (you may need to turn the client's finger to your right side to be more ergonomic). This step is to reduce product bulk on the left side of the acrylic nail.

•Step 6: Hold one end of the nail file in the palm of your hand with the index finger resting on top and on the visualized central line running vertically through the middle of the nail file. Rub the nail file vertically on top to smooth out the entire length of the acrylic nail. Make sure to rub the nail file and follow the contour of the acrylic nail to evenly smooth out the whole nail surface but still retain the curvature of the dome structure. Aim to reduce product thickness evenly from left side to center area to right side of the acrylic nail.

•A proper artificial nail structure must consist of a flushed and tapered cuticle area which gradually transforms to an Apex (the highest part of the nail – usually at about half length of the natural nail bed) then gradually tapers down toward the free edge. Depending on lengths and client's preference, the thickness of the free edge (the end of the nail tip) should be one to two credit cards thick.

Electric File Filing Procedure

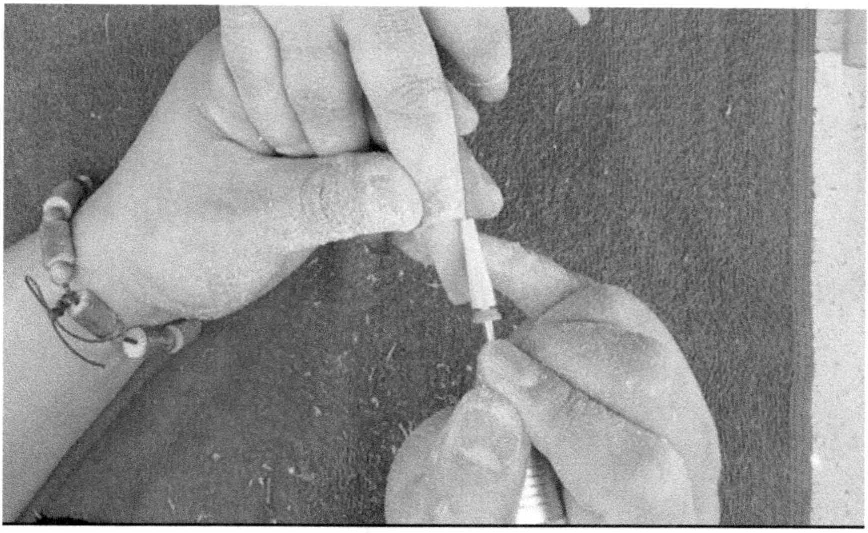

•Step 1: Use the Under Nail Cleaning Bit at 12k to 14k RPM (round per minute) to remove excess powder underneath of the nails and straighten up the side walls.

•Step 2: Use a Diamond Bit or a Cone Shape Cuticle Bit at 8k RPM to clean up, round up and taper the product at the cuticle area. Create a hair line groove to separate the acrylic from the cuticle.

•Step 3: Use a Safety 5-in-1 Fine Carbide Bit or Safety Fine Ceramic Bit at 10k to 12k RPM smooth out Zone 3 of the nail by rubbing the entire body of the nail drill bit back and forth from side to side of the nail.

*NOTE: Divide the entire length of the nail into 3 even parts. Zone 1 is the tip end area. Zone 2 is the central area. Zone 3 is the cuticle and Apex area.

•Step 4: Use vertical strokes to shave down the nail bulk from side to center of each side to create the curvature of the dome structure.

•Step 5: Repeat the side-to-side filing motions of Step 3, but this time gradually move lower and lower from cuticle area down to free edge to smooth out the whole nail length.

•Step 6: Use a 240 Grit Buffer Block to buff smooth the acrylic nails.

Finishing the Nails

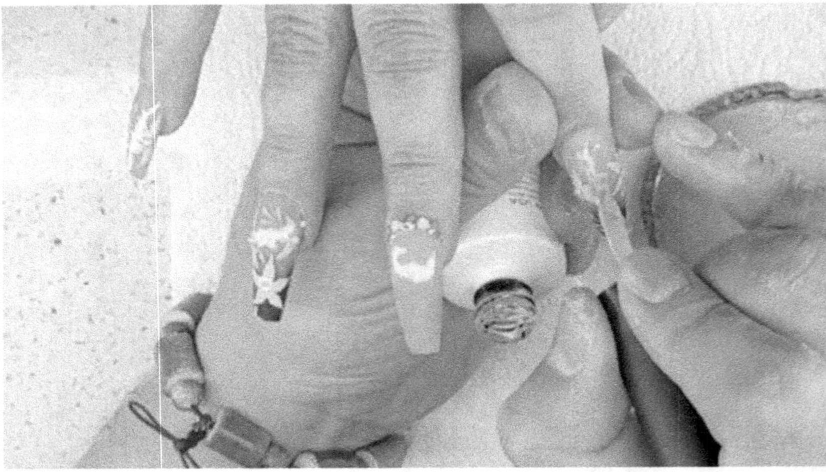

•Step 1: After filing and buffing the nails, let client wash hands with no soap and dry them thoroughly.

•Step 2: Apply either Glossy or Matte LED/UV Gel Topcoat, then cure for 90 seconds in LED/UV gel lamp.

•Step 3: Apply cuticle oil to moisturize and finish sealing the acrylic nails.

•Step 4: Use paper towel to clean the nails and remove excess oil.

•Step 5: Take photos and videos of your work to promote your nail business on different social media platforms.

Nail Photo Samples

Accelerated online nail training
courses at
www.pensight.com/x/lona

Andy Hai Dinh

CHAPTER 2: WORKFLOW TIPS

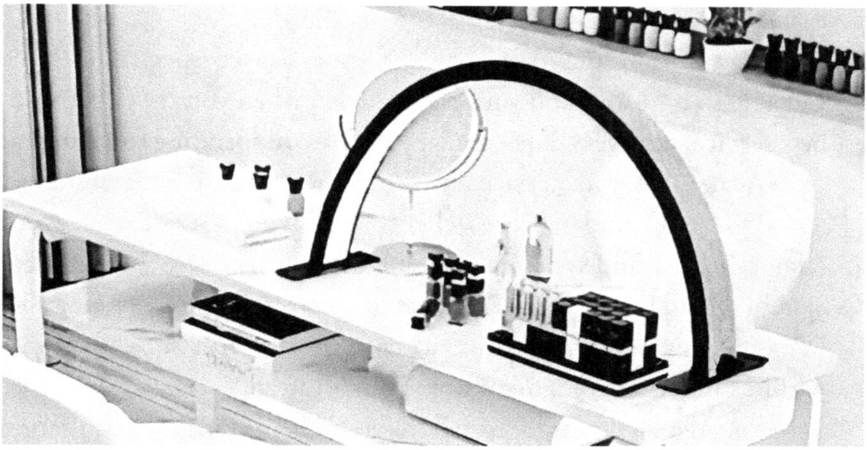

•Organize your nail products, nail art supply, tools, and equipment into separate groups at your workstation and within your reach.

•Systemize your services into step-by-step procedures so that you have a better estimation of how much time you will need to complete each service.

•Stay within the timeframe of your service spectrum. Time is valuable to both you and your clients. Even when you try to provide the best service, not every client will appreciate you spending too much time.

•As in 2024, your service rate should be about $1.50per minute.

•Do not undercharge clients for your services. Create a comprehensive and systemic menu for all your services. Use a "a la carte" system to add prices for all elements of each service. Your pricing should be consistent and competitive in comparison with similar businesses within a proximity of 2 miles from your location.

•Spend a few minutes to talk to your clients during consultation to understand exactly their request. Offer your advice and recommendation during this time, then proceed with the agreed service(s).

•Refrain from engaging too deeply in small talks with clients during servicing time. Instead, offer confirmation by occasionally establishing brief eye contacts and nodding your head.

•It is a great practice to identify the following when booking appointments for your clients:

- What kind of nail service(s) they request

- If they can send you an example photo of the nails they would like to get.

- If they have any existing

artificial nail product on their nails prior to the service.

- How much time they will

be available to get their nails done.

•If clients need a new set of nails and have fake nails on when they come in to see you, proceed with trimming and filing down the artificial enhancements. Then help them to choose the new nail product and serve them complementary drinks while they soak their fake nails in warm Acetone for removal.

•Prioritize Safety over Speed:

If you must stop in the middle of a service to administer First Aid when you injure a client, you will lose a significant amount of time. So, work with your comfortable speed – do not get anxious and try to rush the process. Remember that practice makes perfect. Slow down to apply nail tips perfectly and safely trim or file them into desired shape. Slow down and perfect your product application to reduce the amount of filing after. Start slow and you will finish with a bang!

CHAPTER 3: BUSINESS TIPS

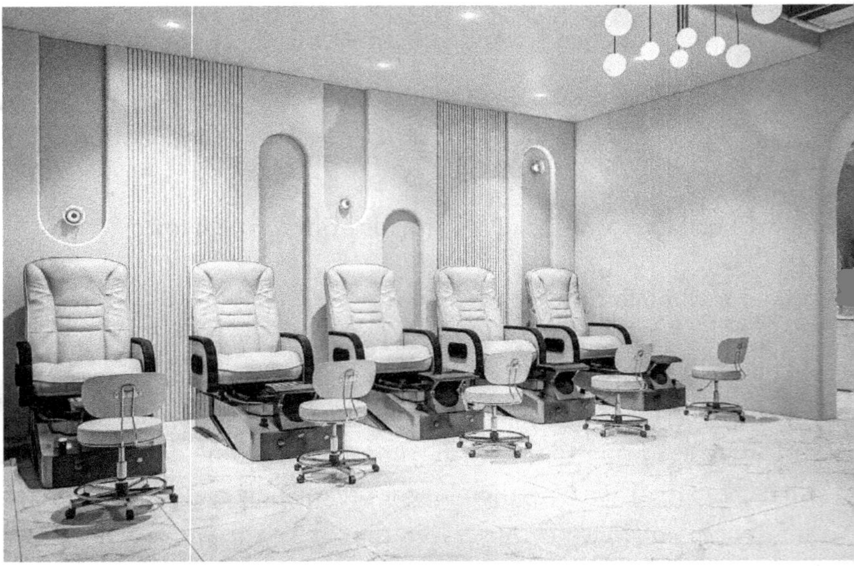

•Owning a successful nail
business is both an art and a science.

•With a dash of innovation, a pinch of hard work, and a commitment to delivering an unforgettable experience, you can set your business apart from the crowd and achieve long-term success.

•Your clients' journey begins the moment they step inside your salon. So always greet your clients with a smile and welcoming body language.

•The top nail businesses always craft an ambiance that makes clients feel like VIPs, starting from the cordial welcome to the final goodbye.

•Invest in your professional development. Utilize premium quality products and provide variety of services to accommodate your client's needs.

•Client contentment is essential to the success of your salon, so strive to always go beyond their expectations.

•Maintain hygiene: Always prioritize cleanliness to ensure a safe and sanitary environment for both you and your clients.

•Stay updated: Keep abreast of the latest nail trends, techniques, and products to offer diverse and up-to-date services.

•Communication is key: Clearly communicate with clients to understand their preferences, address concerns, and manage expectations.

•Time management: Efficiently manage your time to provide quality services without unnecessary delays.

•Nail health first: Prioritize the health of your clients' nails. Educate them on proper care and recommend suitable products.

•Invest in quality tools and equipment: High-quality tools and equipment contribute to better results and a more professional image.

•Develop a personal style:
While staying current with trends, also develop your own unique style to set yourself apart in the industry.

•Marketing savvy: Utilize social media and other platforms to showcase your work, attract clients, and build your brand recognition.

•Continuous learning: Attend trade shows, workshops, conferences, and training sessions to stay updated on new nail techniques and technologies.

•Build client relationships: Foster positive relationships with your clients through excellent service and a friendly demeanor to encourage repeat business and referrals.

•Expense Tracking: Keep a detailed record of all expenses, including supplies, rent, utilities, and any other operational costs. This helps in identifying areas where you can cut costs or optimize spending.

•Profit Margins: Understand your profit margins on different services. Focus on promoting and offering services with higher profit margins to boost overall financial health.

•Inventory Management: Efficiently manage your nail polish, gels, acrylic powders, and other supplies to minimize waste and avoid overstocking.

•Regularly review and update your inventory to align with customer preferences.

•Work Productivity: Monitor your own productivity and ensure you are delivering services in a timely manner. Efficient use of time can positively impact both customer satisfaction and overall revenue.

•Marketing ROI: Evaluate the return on investment (ROI) for your marketing efforts. Focus on strategies that bring in new clients or encourage repeat business. Utilize social media platforms and local advertising wisely.

•Customer Retention: Building a loyal customer base is more cost-effective than constantly acquiring new clients. Implement loyalty programs or promotions to encourage repeat business and referrals. But most importantly, aim to deliver the best customer service and technical excellency.

•Online Presence: Enhance your online presence with a user-friendly website and active social media profiles. Showcase your works, client testimonials, and promotions to attract a broader audience. Utilize paid promotions and advertisement to boost traffic for your business.

•Diversification: Explore additional revenue streams, such as retailing nail care products, organizing workshops, or collaborating with local businesses. Diversification can help stabilize income.

•Create an annual membership program which offers a fixed discounted percentage for all services to utilize clients' membership payments and invest that capitol in retail nail care items which will be sold at your salon by the manager and the staff.

•Legal and Tax Compliance: Stay updated on local business regulations and tax obligations. Failure to comply can result in financial penalties. Consider consulting with a professional accountant to ensure proper compliance.

•Remember, maintaining a strong financial foundation is crucial for the success and sustainability of your nail business.

•Diversify your business capitol by investing 1/3 of your profit into other markets such as real estate, high-yield investment accounts, or other forms of business.

CHAPTER 4: CUSTOMER SERVICE TIPS

•Active Listening: Pay close attention to customers, show empathy, and restate their concerns to demonstrate understanding.

•Prompt Responses: Aim for quick and timely responses to customer inquiries or issues to show that you value their time.

•Clear Communication: Provide information in a clear and concise manner, avoiding jargon, to ensure customers understand your responses.

•Solution-Oriented: Focus on finding solutions rather than dwelling on problems. Offer alternatives and work towards resolving issues effectively.

•Always respond promptly to all reviews. Sincerely give thanks to positive reviews and acknowledge clients' royalty. Extend invitations for clients to invite their loved ones, friends, and co-workers to your salon.

•Friendly and publicly respond to negative reviews with requests for clients to directly contact salon manager for remedy or solutions. Most clients will be satisfied if you offer them to come back for a discounted or free service and willing to update their negative reviews to positive reviews which will earn trustworthiness for your business from other potential clients.

•Personalization: Address customers by their names and tailor your responses based on their specific situations, making them feel valued and understood.

•Positive Language: Use positive and reassuring language to create a friendly atmosphere, even when addressing challenges or complaints.

•Apologize Sincerely: If there's an issue, apologize genuinely, taking responsibility and assuring the customer that you're committed to resolving the problem.

•Follow-Up: After resolving an issue, follow up to ensure the customer is satisfied and inquire if there's anything else you can assist them with.

•Product Knowledge: Be well-versed in your products or services to provide accurate information and guide customers effectively.

•Learn from Feedback: Embrace feedback, whether positive or negative, as an opportunity to improve and enhance the customer experience.

•Patience: Stay patient, especially in challenging situations. Keep in mind that a calm and composed response is essential for customer satisfaction.

•Go the Extra Mile: Surprising customers with unexpected gestures, like discounts or additional information to exceed their expectations and foster loyalty.

•As an individual service provider or a business, aim to build a personal relationship with each client. Make them feel that coming to see you for nail services is not just a necessity but also a therapeutic treatment.

•Remember, providing excellent customer service is not just about resolving issues but also about creating a positive and memorable experience for your customers.

CHAPTER 5: STARTING A NAIL SALON BUSINESS

•Market Research: Understand your target market, local competition, and potential customer base.

•Business Plan: Outline your salon's concept, services offered, target market, and financial projections.

•Business Structure: Choose a legal structure (e.g., sole proprietorship, LLC) and register your business.

•Permits and Licenses: Check and obtain the necessary licenses and permits for operating a salon in your area.

•Depending on each US jurisdiction but in general, to open or build a nail salon, you will need to obtain the following paperwork:

-Lease Agreement
-Establishment Blueprint
-Zoning Permit
-Business License
-Business Insurance Policy
-Establishment License
-Professional License
-Health Permit
-Fire Department Inspection

•Choose a Location: Select a strategic location with good visibility, accessibility, and plenty of parking spaces. Prime locations are often within proximity of a shopping mall, a business district, large retailers such as Walmart or Target, or main intersections of major freeways.

•Salon Design: Create an appealing and comfortable interior that aligns with your brand.

•Nail Care Equipment: Purchase high-quality nail care stations, chairs, and equipment.

•Supplies: Stock up on a variety of nail products, tools, and other supplies.

•Create a comprehensive service menu for your nail salon. Clearly define the services you'll offer, such as manicures, pedicures, acrylic nails, nail art, waxing, lashes, etc.

•Set Pricing: Establish competitive and reasonable pricing for your services.

•Hire Skilled Staff: Recruit licensed and skilled nail technicians.

•In-house Training: Provide ongoing training to keep your staff updated on the latest trends and techniques.

•Create a Brand: Develop a unique brand identity for your salon. A great brand name should be short, unique, and easy to remember.

•Marketing Plan: Utilize online (Facebook, Instagram, Google Ads) and offline (loyalty program, membership program, word-of-mouth referrals, local business listing, flyers) marketing strategies to promote your salon.

•Online Booking: Utilize online booking systems such as: GlossGenius, Square, Acuity Scheduling, Mindbody, Fresha, Vagaro, or Booksy.

•Website: Create a professional website with information about your services, pricing, and contact details.

•Social Media: Use social media platforms such as Facebook, Instagram and TikTok to showcase your work, engage with customers, and promote special offers.

•Focus on Customer Service: Provide excellent customer service to build loyalty and positive word-of-mouth.

CHAPTER 6: NAIL SALON BUDGETING

Creating a budget for your nail salon business is crucial for financial stability and success.

Here's an outlined guide for your salon budgeting:

Startup Costs

•Lease/Rent: Include the cost of securing a location for your salon.

•Renovation/Interior Design:

Budget for any necessary renovations or interior design to create an appealing salon space.

•Licenses and Permits: Account for fees associated with obtaining the required licenses and permits.

•Equipment and Furniture: Estimate costs for nail care stations, spa chairs, chairs, manicure tables, cabinets, bathroom fixtures, lighting fixtures, decorations, and other necessary equipment.

•Initial Inventory: Allocate funds for an initial supply of nail products, tools, cleaning supplies and other salon essentials.

Operational Expenses

•Utilities: Include monthly expenses for electricity, water, heating, and cooling.

•Salon Supplies: Budget for ongoing purchases of nail products, acetone, cotton balls, and other consumables.

•Staff Salaries: Allocate funds for the salaries or hourly wages of your nail technicians and support staff.

•Marketing and Advertising: Set aside a budget for promotional materials, online marketing, and advertising campaigns.

•Insurance: Include costs for business insurance to protect your salon against unforeseen events.

•Training and Development:

Allocate funds for ongoing training and professional development for your staff.

Miscellaneous Expenses

•Cleaning Services: If needed, budget for professional cleaning services.

•Decor and Ambiance: Set aside funds for maintaining and updating the salon's décor to keep it fresh and inviting.

•Maintenance: Account for the regular maintenance and repair of salon equipment.

Contingency Fund

•Emergency Fund: Allocate a percentage of your budget for unexpected expenses or economic downturns.

Revenue and Profit Goals

•Sales Projections: Estimate your monthly and yearly sales based on your pricing structure and expected customer traffic.

•Profit Margin: Set realistic profit margin goals to ensure sustainability and growth.

Regularly review and adjust your budget as needed, especially during the early stages of your business. This will help you stay financially organized and make informed decisions to achieve your salon's success.

Consider consulting with a financial advisor or accountant for more personalized guidance.

Ensure a detailed budget, manage expenses wisely, build a loyal client base through promotions, and stay updated on industry trends to enhance services and attract more customers.

CONCLUSION

In concluding this guidebook, embarking on the journey of establishing and managing a successful nail salon business requires a delicate balance of creativity, professionalism, and strategic planning.

By meticulously navigating the crucial steps outlined

here – from initial research and legal considerations to creating a vibrant atmosphere and providing top-notch services – you lay the foundation for a thriving business venture.

Remember, each satisfied customer contributes to the growth of your salon. Stay attuned to industry trends, continuously refine your skills, and foster a culture of exceptional customer service.

As you embark on this exciting endeavor, may your nail salon not only flourish but become a haven of beauty and relaxation, leaving an indelible mark in the hearts and beautiful nails of your valued clientele.

Here's to the success of your nail salon business!

Andy Hai Dinh

Books By This Author

•Acrylic and Dipping Powder - Product Knowledge and Applications (publication year: 2023)

•The Nail technician's Career Guide (publication year: 2023)

•A Beginner's Guide to Trading - Stock and Forex Technical Analysis (publication year: 2025)

•WIN MORE, TRADE BETTER - A Practical Guide to Trading and Investing (publication year: 2025)

Watch for more at "pensight.com/x/lona".

Don't miss out!

Visit the website below and you can sign up to receive emails whenever Andy Hai Dinh publishes a new book. There's no charge and no obligation.

https://books2read.com/r/B-A-YYJBB-KFVQC

BOOKS 2 READ

Connecting independent readers to independent writers.

Also by Andy Hai Dinh

Acrylic and Dipping Powder - Product Knowledge and Applications
The Nail technician's Career Guide
A Beginner's Guide to Trading - Stock and Forex Technical Analysis
Win More, Trade Better - A Practical Guide to Trading and Investing
Win More, Trade Better - A Practical Guide to Trading and Investing

Watch for more at https://pensight.com/x/lona.

About the Author

Andy Hai Dinh is a market researcher and business consultant in the beauty industry. He is also a part-time trader profiting from swing trading stocks and Forex currencies.

www.ingramcontent.com/pod-product-compliance
Lightning Source LLC
LaVergne TN
LVHW022319200926
848481LV00004B/1376

* 9 7 9 8 2 2 3 3 6 7 6 6 6 *